Triumphant

Freda Higgins

Triumphant

REFLECTIONS ON
THE HEALING POWER OF LOVE
IN A FAMILY'S STRUGGLE
WITH LEUKEMIA

FREDA HIGGINS

Zonani Books,
Reedville, VA

The Holy Bible scriptural quotation sources:
NIV—New International Version® © 1973,1978, 1984, 2011
by Biblica, Inc.™ Used by permission. All rights reserved worldwide.
CEV—Contemporary English Version © 1991, 1992, 1995
by American Bible Society. Used by permission.
ESV—English Standard Version® (ESV®) © by Crossway, a publishing ministry of
Good News Publishers. Used by permission. All rights reserved.

For permission to reproduce selections of this book please contact:

FREDA HIGGINS
P.O. Box 373
Reedville, VA 22539
email: zoey@kaballero.com

Printed in the USA

ISBN: 978-0-9856099-0-0 paperback

Book and cover design by Richard Stodart

In Loving Memory Of

Joshua
&
Elizabeth

And all of the children we
have met along the way

*See, I am sending an Angel before you to guard you along
the way and to bring you to the place I have prepared.*

Exodus 23:20 (NIV)

Over the years, God has moved our family through a journey that we would never have chosen to travel. I can tell you that we were carried by Him through our darkest days. I can also testify to His great wisdom, power and love. He gave us the miracle we all prayed for of letting Michael stay with us. Even the doctor's say they witnessed a miracle! God has humbled us through Michael and all of the children we have met and some we have lost along the way; they brought love and compassion to people's lives. Each one of these children will remain with me all the days of my life.

Many of you have gone to great effort and inconvenience to give us time in our hour of need that you could have spent with your own families.

We want to thank you, our own family and friends, and people who didn't even know our family, for all you have meant to us during this journey. You have lifted us up to Him in prayer as we felt His very presence upon us. We want you all to know we love and appreciate you in such a manner that is overwhelming.

CONTENTS

This is a story about a family whose child was diagnosed with Leukemia. The entire family struggled to overcome the obstacles they faced.

My hope is that it will give other families facing this difficult journey the faith and will to conquer any obstacle in their path without despair.

Although Michael faced a life threatening disease, he showed us how to come through it with his faith stronger than ever.

Michael is a courageous young man who chose to fight against cancer with Jesus by his side and the love of his family.

Against all odds, he is "Triumphant."

Freda Higgins

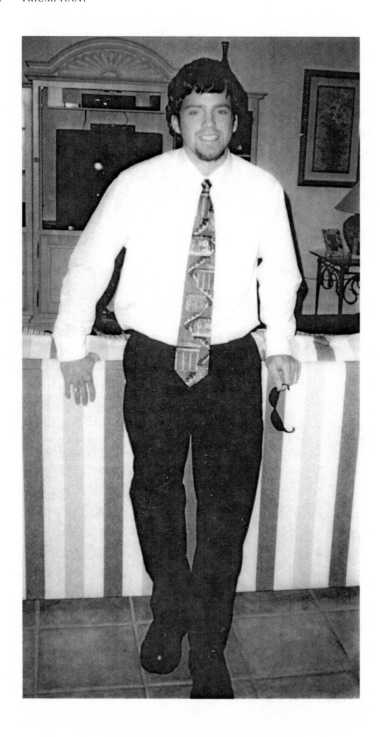

1

On February 5, 1997, I was in the kitchen making my usual morn-ing cup of coffee when I heard someone at the front door. When I opened it, there stood Michael, my sixteen-year-old son. I thought he had already gotten on the school bus. He looked very pale, al-most blue in color, and asked if he could stay home from school that day.

"What's wrong?" I asked.

"I just feel really tired, and if I don't lie down I think I will fall down," he replied.

I helped him up the stairs to his room. Michael slept most of that day.

That evening, we decided to go by the clinic to have him checked out to see if he was anemic. I had taken Michael to the doctor the past year for numerous ailments, such as bronchitis, inflammation of the ribs, and many colds.

When the doctor came in, he looked at Michael, examined him, squeezed his fingertips with a very puzzled look on his face, and then ordered blood work. Before he left the room, he said, "Something is terribly wrong. This does not look good."

I felt as if I had a hole in my stomach when I heard the doctor's words. Michael looked over at me with a very serious look on his face and said, "I hope I don't have cancer."

When the doctor entered the examination room again, he said, "This could be a couple of things." He named off a few, like mono and anemia. I was stunned to hear the final one: Leukemia.

2

Michael Bandon Miller, my first child, was born on March 6, 1980, at 1:20 p.m. in Winchester, Virginia, weighing in at eight pounds and one ounce. My husband Jerry and I took him home, and we began our lives together in a little town called Berryville, Virginia.

We lived in a townhouse facing an apple orchard. Sometimes we would sit in our living room and watch the cows in the orchard eating the fallen apples. It was a beautiful place to raise children.

Michael was a happy little boy growing up, and very healthy. We bonded very closely, as sons and mothers often do. I had no inkling back then just how much we would come to need each other.

Although Michael's father and I divorced when he was three years old, it did not appear to affect Michael, who always had a smile on his face in all of the pictures I took of him growing up.

On one occasion during this time, Michael was playing with a little six-year-old boy who lived next door. It was getting late, and I went to get him. The family was having dinner, but Michael was not there!

"Where's Michael?" I asked.

The boy replied, "He was playing over by the woods beside our house."

I ran out the door and through the woods calling for him. I remember feeling panic as it was becoming dusk outside. All kinds of things raced through my mind.

"Where are you? Where are you?" I screamed.

I could feel the acid rushing into my stomach. Everyone joined in the search. On a hunch, I went around the back of our townhouse and looked down through the parking lot. There was Michael sitting on a curb, playing with his truck in the dirt without a care in the world.

Although he gave me a big scare that day, oh, how I would now give anything for him not have a care in the world again.

I know in my heart that although I cannot see them, there is likely a circle of angels surrounding and protecting Michael all the time.

On another occasion, while running outside he fell and hit his face on the concrete. When I picked him up his gums were deep purple in color, but he did not lose his teeth! What a tough little boy he was!

When Michael was five years old, we sold our townhouse and moved to Maryland, were I married my husband, Randy. We lived at first with his wonderful parents, Betty and Louie, who treated us like family from the beginning. I was not surprised to see Michael bond so closely with them.

Eventually, we built our family home in Laurel, Maryland, where Michael developed strong bonds with new friends.

I gave birth to Randy Mathew, my second son, on July 12, 1988. My husband brought Michael to visit us in the hospital. When it was time to leave, baby Randy had his tiny hand wrapped tightly around Michael's finger. Michael looked at us with large tears in his big green eyes and said, with a trembling lip and a quiver in his voice, "He doesn't want me to leave!"

When we were released from the hospital my mother-in-law, Betty, and my sister-in-law, Shelby, took us home.

My boys developed a deep love for one another. Michael was Randy's big brother, and was always very protective of him.

When Michael was in middle school, he was on the basketball team. He loved playing basketball and was good at it.

On the day before Thanksgiving, I had gone out to pick up our fresh turkey. When I returned home, there were numerous phone messages for me. The school had been trying to reach me.

Michael had been playing basketball, and when he was coming down from making a shot another boy had jumped up to block him. Here we go again! The top of the boy's head hit Michael in the mouth, and they both fell to the floor. The boy was dazed from the impact to his head, and Michael was stunned for a few seconds. He thought he was fine, until he saw blood on his shirt and on the floor. When he put his hands up to his face, he realized that his teeth had folded back into the roof of his mouth! Without hesitation, Michael reached in and pulled his teeth back down.

The school was not able to reach me, so they called his emergency contact. When I was able to call the school, they explained everything to me. I met the other parent with Michael at the dentist's office, where they cemented bracing to his teeth so they would not move. Michael still has his teeth to this day because he acted so quickly. I have always called Michael my 'old soul' because he is so wise beyond his years. He has taught me so much about the power of God's love...and I realize now it all started the day that he was born.

Although it was hard for Michael to leave his high school and friends, in 1996 we sold our house and moved to Fredericksburg, Virginia, where most of my family lived. We all left behind many great friends with whom bonds will never be broken.

My in-laws, Betty and Louie, also moved to Fredericksburg, since

Randy and his father Louie were in business together. Looking back, it may all have been in God's plan that we all be together as a family so that we could be supported during Michael's ordeal.

Michael soon made new friends and started going to church. My family never taught us about God, reading the bible, or going to church. I have a close friend I talked to about this, and how I felt an empty place inside me. I could never explain it, but I'd become sad and almost depressed and did not know why. Now I know that I was missing faith, hope, and the love that comes with knowing Jesus. All this changed because Michael led us to Him. I feel the power and the love of the Lord.

Although they are eight years apart, Michael and Randy were close from the beginning, and Michael liked pulling pranks on his brother. One particular incident stands out in my mind as an example of Michael's sense of humor.

We had two phone lines in our house. One was the in-home business office phone at the back of the house. One day, Michael used it to call our other number, and his brother Randy answered the telephone.

"Hello," said Randy.

"Is Robby there?" asked Michael.

"I think you have the wrong phone number," answered Randy.

"Ok, thanks," replied Michael, and hung up. He waited a couple of months before he called again. Randy answered, and Michael asked for Robby again in a deep scruffy voice.

"You have the wrong number," Randy again replied and hung up. Michael called back immediately and asked for Robby again! Randy was beginning to feel uncomfortable talking with this person, so he tried to hand the phone to me saying, "Mom! This person keeps calling for Robby!"

All along I knew who it really was on the other end of the line, but I said with a straight face, "Tell him he has the wrong number."

"I did mom!" Randy said with frustration, "But he keeps calling back!"

Reluctantly, he told the person on the other end that it was the wrong number and hung up.

It was hard not to laugh! Michael was in tears from laughing so hard in the other room. When he heard Randy coming down the hallway, he ran quickly to the bathroom and put a washcloth over his face to hide his laughter, pretending instead that he was washing it.

Randy came in with a wide-eyed look on his face and said,

"You will never guess who just called! It was that guy asking for Robby again, and I think he is losing his voice!"

Michael never called again after that day.

Although Michael did well in school and loved playing basketball, we were unaware that he started sleeping through most of his classes and on the bus. His legs and knees also started aching, so he stopped playing basketball. We thought that this was just due to 'growing pains'. His friends became concerned. They asked him at school if he was feeling okay. Michael remembers his art teacher talking to him and asking him if something was wrong. Her voice sounded to him as if she were in a tunnel. Michael remembers replying jokingly, "I probably have cancer."

All of this seems like yesterday. But it was actually over fifteen years ago on February 5, 1997, when Michael was diagnosed with Acute Lymphoblastic Leukemia (A.L.L.).

Acute Lymphoblastic Leukemia, or cancer, is caused by the over-production of immature white blood cells (also termed "blast") continuously multiplying and over-producing in the bone marrow. A.L.L. causes death by crowding out normal cells in the bone marrow, and by spreading (metastasizing) to other organs. The symptoms are often associated with anemia. Patients can tire easily and have aching in the bones and joints and just not be feeling well, all of which Michael was experiencing. It can be fatal in as little as a few weeks if left untreated.

The doctor sent us to Mary Washington Hospital in Fredericksburg, Virginia. After the hospital ran their tests, they told me that there was a possibility that Michael might have leukemia. When I called my husband Randy at work and told him that Michael might have cancer, he thought that I might be joking. While he was driving to the hospital, my words sank in and he began to wonder what was going to happen to Michael.

He had no idea just how much this would impact so many lives.

The doctors placed a mask over Michael's face. His immune system had become so compromised that the slightest germ or virus he came in contact with could jeopardize him further. At that point, the doctors advised us to take him straight to the University of Virginia Hospital where a medical team was waiting for us.

Our whole family was at our house waiting for news. When my brother Mike heard that Michael had cancer, he said that he could not find the words to describe his feelings. "It can't be," he thought, actually feeling sick to his stomach. Then his thoughts turned to my husband Randy, Randy Mathew, and me. He could not imagine how or what we were all going through. He thought to himself that the pain he was experiencing could not compare to what we were feeling as parents. Mike just wanted to take all of our hurt and pain away, however he possibly could.

My sister, Nancy, who was always close to Michael, stepped in to take care of young Randy while we were gone. Michael had spent many nights with Nancy and his cousins growing up, and loved being with them. It was like a second home for him. When Nancy first heard the news, she said that it was as if something evil had swept in and ripped out her heart. It left her, and everyone else, feeling paralyzed. She knew that we were all about to begin a long journey with Michael.

This disease would cause so much pain to our hearts and souls.

Then eight years old, Randy Mathew recalls how he learned that Michael was sick. He had already been in bed for hours because it was a school night. A family member had awakened him, and in a "blur" he had shuffled to the bottom of the steps to find the entire family gathered in our home. He remembers hearing bits and pieces of something going on about his brother, but nothing definitive. Even so, he knew that something was terribly wrong with Michael. When his aunt gave him the news in the morning he remembers feeling crushed. The pain he felt was "unreal."

Everything was happening so fast. I think we were all in shock.

"This cannot be happening!" I thought to myself as we drove together along the road to the hospital in Charlottesville.

I recall how dark and winding the road was, and how it seemed to go on forever. My husband told me to pay attention and get to know my way to the hospital because I would be traveling that route frequently. I turned around often to look at Michael, asking him if he was doing all right. He just nodded. I could not imagine what he must be feeling. At times, I could not even speak for fear of totally breaking down, and I didn't want to scare Michael any more than he already was. I kept thinking to myself, please dear God, let us wake up from this horrible nightmare.

During the hour and thirty minutes it took to get to the hospital, Michael did not say a word. When we arrived at the emergency room, the doctors and nurses were waiting for him. They rushed him straight back to run their own tests. The tests indicated that Michael's organs were shutting down. His white cells were taking over, and he did not have enough red blood cells to carry oxygen to all of his organs.

Oh, how things can change in an instant!

Still reeling from the news, we now faced the decision to start him on chemotherapy right away. The doctors went over all of the drugs that he would be given: Methotrexate is a drug that inhibits cellular reproduction; Vincristine is used to treat leukemia by blocking cell division. It is also highly toxic; Daunorubicin is an anti-cancer drug that kills cancer cells; Leucovorin is used to help prevent harmful effects of the methotrexate; Methylprednisolone is a steroid used to provide relief for inflamed areas of the body. It also lessens swelling, redness, itching, and allergic reactions; Ara-C is injected directly into the spinal fluid because the central nervous system (brain) is a site that chemotherapy drugs cannot penetrate. Consequently, this part of the body as a result becomes a reservoir for leukemia cells. Without this treatment, there is a chance in some patients of having a 'relapse' of the leukemia in their brain; Mercaptopurine is an immunosuppressive drug used to prevent the formation and spread of cancer cells.

These were just a few of the drugs given to Michael. All of them have side effects, including nausea and vomiting, loss of appetite, skin rashes, hair loss, muscle weakness, mouth sores, bone pain, kidney toxicity, and they may affect the heart, brain and organs. Moreover, even after enduring all of the unpleasant side effects, Michael could still die. Although it was a small percentage who did, it still dwelled in the back of my mind after reading about it.

Because Michael's biological father lived in Florida and had not yet arrived at the hospital, I had to sign papers giving my permission to start the treatment. I remember being afraid of losing Michael, yet scared to sign those papers. They were about to pump poison into his veins to kill cancer cells. Nevertheless, it seemed to be our only alternative or we would surely lose him. Although I was terrified, I tried reassuring Michael that everything would be fine.

The nurse started the intravenous fluids, and the treatment started. Michael just lay there in a state of shock and looking very pale.

When I met my family waiting outside his hospital room the next day, I did not think that Michael could hear us since I had to pass through two sets of doors to get to them. It turned out that he could. Later, he told me that it really did not register with him just how serious his illness was until he heard me break down outside his room. I had let everything I was really feeling come pouring out as I collapsed into my dad's arms. I just could not hold back the overwhelming feelings any longer. Michael understood then just how serious his situation was, because in the sixteen years of his life he had never heard me cry like that. My sister Nancy said my cries filled the hall, and knew then that our lives would be forever altered.

Michael experienced many difficulties, and remained in the hospital for a month. Some of the drugs he was given made him feel like he was suspended in air, spinning and turning over. Others made his whole body jerk uncontrollably. Michael also contracted pneumonia, and he had such a violent cough that he developed double hernias. The doctors repaired them, and after he healed he was given a discharge date. I stayed with him the entire time, only returning home to prepare for his homecoming. Michael had quite a few visits from friends and family, and many people had begun praying for him. There were prayers for him from as far as California.

3

I remember the trip home. It wasn't the long, dark, and winding road that it had seemed to be going to the hospital. The day was sunny and bright, and it was actually a beautiful drive. I think I cried the whole way, only this time from happiness. Michael was finally coming home after surviving such a serious condition.

A song by the group Alabama came over the radio, "I believe there are angels among us." I believe that we are all given signs of this in our life. We just have to stop, listen, and look around to see them. I could hardly believe Michael had survived all of this.

During the stay at the hospital, we had the pleasure of meeting some wonderful people. Some were patients and their families, while others were doctors and nurses. Like the song that was playing said, "they came to me in my darkest hours." I believe that God had sent angels to help us get through this, "to guide us with the light of love."

That was the moment that I started praying for the strength just to make it through the tough times. I did not ask for miracles—just strength for Michael, myself, and our family.

God thinks highly of you, and at the very moment you started
praying, I was sent to give you the answer.

DANIEL 9:23 (CEV)

Michael was so excited to be going home. When we arrived, there was a large banner stretched across our house, "Welcome Home Michael!" and lots of balloons. Everyone was happy to have him back, but no one could have been more grateful to be home than Michael!

Michael was now very thin, weak, and frail from the chemotherapy. He had lost most of his muscle mass, and could not walk well. Still, he wanted to see his room so badly that he started crawling up the steps. My husband Randy helped him up the steps. When he got to his room, he fell on the bed with his arms wide open and cried, "I love my room!"

A few weeks went by, and Michael began losing hair from the chemo. The hair was in his bed, on his clothes, and when he took showers it covered him. So one day I held up a comb and a pair of shears. Michael's hair was long, so this was going to be new for us. Under the circumstances, he decided that if it had to go we would have some fun with it. I took the electric shears and started cutting. I cut off the top of his hair down to his ears and left the rest long. He put on a pair of glasses and walked around like an old man. We laughed so hard that day. We finished by shaving off what used to be dark, thick, wavy hair that had become thin and stringy. I think it was harder for me. As each piece of hair dropped to the floor, tears ran down my face. It wasn't just the hair, it was just that it was one more thing that was being taken away from him. But he said that it was only hair, and that it would grow back. Little did we know how it would come back in different colors and textures every time he lost it! We would joke around and tell him that he could be in the witness protection program with all his different looks!

As the weeks went by, young Randy was not feeling well. He complained that his legs hurt. I panicked, and took him to the doctor for a wide range of tests. Everything came back normal. What an enormous relief that was!

We had to make trips back to the clinic in Charlottesville, Virginia, that year for spinal taps, tests and other lab work. Michael remembers the harrowing ordeal of his first bone marrow aspiration during the first admission. He had not had enough sedation and had felt the whole procedure. He lay there clenching his teeth in silence. He was not one to complain about anything.

He was in and out of the hospital for different ailments. Because his immune system was so compromised and weak from all of the chemotherapy, we had to be aware of who was around him at all times. We had to screen everyone who came for visits to make sure they were not sick or had any live virus vaccines. He couldn't receive flowers, and I could not have houseplants. Since dirt carries a certain amount of bacteria, I didn't even work in the flowerbeds. Everyone took their shoes off at the door. I was constantly wiping things with disinfectant. I felt at times that I just wanted to put him into a bubble to keep him safe.

Michael had a central line placed in his chest that went straight into an artery. These lines prevent the chemo drugs from burning the veins and provide overnight nutrition, which he had to have because he was so thin and did not have an appetite. As a foreign object placed in the body, the line was susceptible to bacterial infections. Therefore, whenever an infection occurred, his doctor would have to remove the line until the infection cleared up with antibiotics and then replace it with a new one. Needless to say, Michael had quite a few scars on his chest.

We lived an hour and thirty minutes from the hospital in Charlottesville. If his temperature went past 101, we went straight in because his immune system was so weak that any infection could have run rampant through his body.

I remember there were times that we had to make the drive through snowstorms. There was no other choice. We simply had to do it. Before we left, I always prayed to the Lord to just get him there safely. Even though we saw four-wheel drive vehicles in the ditches and cars sliding all over the road, somehow we made it in my little sports car! I felt as if my shoulders were pulling into my neck, yet we made it!

Sometimes, we would have to leave in the middle of the night and during those trips in particular that road seemed long, dark and lonely. Although we saw many deer on the roadside, I prayed..."just let me get him there." We never hit any animals! (Thank you, Saint Francis!)

Our relatives and friends were amazing! Betty and Louie often helped take care of Randy Mathew. When we needed them, they were always there for us. They kept busy doing fundraisers to help cover some of the medical expenses. All of my sisters and sisters-in-law, my brother and brothers-in-law, nieces and nephews, mothers and fathers worked so hard. I cannot express the gratitude and love I feel for them. They even stood in the middle of highways asking for donations. They sold baked goods, sponsored concerts, and held a dance in Michael's honor. Total strangers gave not only money but also their time to Michael. May God bless every one of those people!

A year later, tests were done to see if he was in remission. Yes! He had succeeded!

To commemorate this wonderful news, Michael even got a tattoo across his shoulders that described how he felt, "TRIUMPHANT." It felt so good to live again, to see Michael again at home reclaiming his life.

Michael was able to finish school and graduate with his class of 1998.

4

Michael started work at a new job and life returned to normal. He got another tattoo on his left forearm, of Jesus holding the world in his hands. Michael said he put great thought into this, and that it was a constant reminder to him that Jesus was always with him no matter what he faced. I remember when the nurses were having a difficult time drawing blood from his right arm that they would look at his left and pause. They had a problem sticking Jesus!

Michael had also started back to school at the local college. He was almost ready for finals, when he came to me one day with a swollen testicle. So back we went to the hospital.

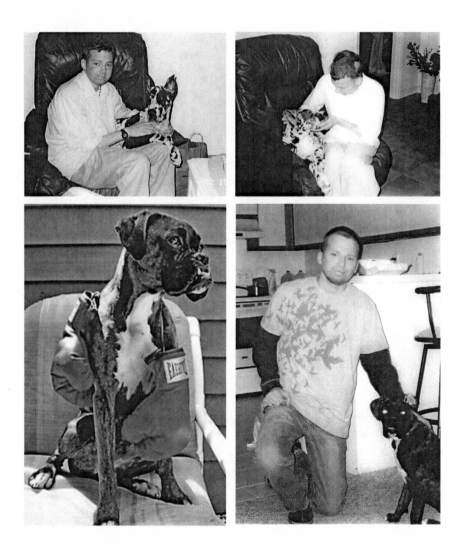

5

The doctor examined Michael and ordered another spinal tap. Just as we feared, the leukemia was back. Michael had relapsed.

Cancer can be devious and elusive. Unfortunately, it hides in the testicles of males. Michael needed localized radiation to his testicles. His doctor explained to him about radiation and that he would not be able to father any children after he had it. He immediately looked over at me with a clinched jaw. Tears of disappointment streamed down his face. He told me later it broke his heart because he knew I had always looked forward to having grandchildren.

Oh, how my heart was hurting for him! It was often hard to hold back the tears. I had to step into the hall to clear the lump in my throat. Although I had a deep sadness in my heart, I reassured him it would be all right. There was always the option for him to adopt a child. There were children out there who needed parents, and we would love them just the same as if they were his own.

The doctor had been giving him more bad news and all he was thinking about was my loss. I told him then that as long as he was all right, I would be too.

My connection with Michael was so strong that even when we

were not together I could feel him and his pain. The strangest thing that I recall is that I developed a callus on my lower back. When I showed it to Michael's doctor, she could not believe what she saw. The callus was exactly where Michael had received all of his spinal taps!

I tried sitting in on some of the taps, but looking at the size of the needle and knowing it was going into his spine for fluid just made me feel faint. I felt that I would pass out, so I just slipped into the hall and waited until it was over.

Michael did not get to finish college because the doctors started another round of chemo. The nurses in the clinic were so good to Michael and to all of the children that came in for chemo treatments, blood work, and spinal taps. These people are truly amazing. They deal with sick children nonstop every day, and I had never once heard them complain. Some children were too young to understand everything that was happening to them. Everyone is so patient and caring.

When the nurses gave Michael the medication to sedate him, his chin and nose would itch. They would just rub his back and make him feel so secure. He would often tease them by snapping a five-dollar bill and saying, "I have a crisp five dollar bill here for some extra meds to make me sleep!" The nurses would just look at him, shake their heads, and laugh.

Michael spent many birthdays and Christmases in the hospital. In fact, I think he spent just about every holiday in the hospital!

I remember one hospital stay just before Christmas. The doctors had told him he would be out before the big day! Days passed, and they kept adding a day, then another day. Well, I guess you know how that goes. Most of the time, he was in good spirits. But this time it got him down.

I received a phone call from the floor nurses that Michael was threatening to leave the hospital! When I got off the elevator and

turned the corner to his room, I was very surprised to see objects being hurled from his room! I had to stop and laugh, since this behavior just was so out of character for Michael. He was always the type instead that nurses would fight over to have as a patient. Throughout the hospital, everyone knew Michael as such a well-mannered patient.

The nurses would try to get blood from his feet because they were unable to access his veins any other place. All of his veins had been used too many times. The needle would go in, but with no luck. They would pull it out and try it repeatedly, moving the needle around in and out. They always feel badly about this and apologized to him for having to put him through it. Michael would always say, "That's ok," and even thank them, wishing them a good day as they were leaving the room. Most of them could not believe that this boy who had missed his teenage years watching his friends move on with their lives while his seemed to be standing still, and who had to face his own mortality at such a young age, could be lying there being so kind to them. However, on that day he had taken all the disappointment that he could manage.

Since Michael was very fond of one nurse, Melissa, she was sent in to calm him down. She just had a way about her and could always put a smile back on his face. Besides, he did not want her to see him upset. And of course, she was always on his side! I imagine that helped quite a bit.

During one of his stays in the hospital, Michael said that something was different when he was receiving one of the chemo drugs. His stomach hurt, so they gave him a drug called Zofran to calm his stomach. I took him home, and late that night I was awakened by a knock at my bedroom door. It was young Randy. We could hear the panic in his voice.

"Michael is lying in the bathroom floor crying," Randy said.

Michael had become violently sick to his stomach, and said that the pain was unbearable. I called his doctor and rushed him back to the hospital! The whole way there, he moaned in pain. He wasn't able to find a position that would give him any relief from the pain. I had never seen him in so much agony. I felt that I could not get him there quickly enough. I was in such a state of panic myself not knowing what was going on with him, that I don't even recall parts of the drive to the hospital!

They took him straight into emergency and began a morphine drip for the pain. He was in so much pain that even the morphine did not work. Michael didn't believe that he had been given anything! But, it ended up being too much morphine, which sent him straight into the Intensive Care Unit. He had been given an overdose and developed an allergic reaction to morphine. The doctors diagnosed Michael with pancreatitis, due to the chemo drug he had received early that day. That was just one of the many side effects L-asparaginase could have. The doctors told us that he had only a one in five chance of even surviving this! The pancreatitis attack had damaged eighty percent of his pancreas. As a result, Michael became insulin-dependent, and would have to give himself insulin shots every day for the rest of his life.

Days went by, and I stayed by his side. Everyone was so upset to hear that he was not doing well, even the nurses. Nurse Melissa stayed outside his door until late in the night crying, because she knew just how serious it was.

My family came, and insisted that I go downstairs to get something to eat and drink, or just take a break. My sister, Nancy, stayed outside the intensive care unit waiting for me to return.

It was a long corridor and she was leaning with her back against the wall as the lights became dim for the evening. She was very distraught over Michael and the possibility of losing him after his coming so far. Then she heard someone come walking down the corridor with a distinct limp and a cane. He walked up to her and leaned beside her. The stranger asked her if she had a loved one in there, and she said "Yes" through her tears. The man gently put his hand on her shoulder and told her how lucky we all are to have Michael and that we were to have faith, for he believed that Michael would pull through.

He will cover you with his feathers, and under his wings you will find refuge.

PSALMS 91:4 (NIV)

The man stood there with Nancy in silence for a while, then turned and walked back down the corridor. Nancy described him as being very caring. The chilling thing for her about their entire exchange was she had never once mentioned Michael's name! How did the stranger know it? I asked around the hospital, but no one had seen the man.

Michael recovered and amazed all the doctors yet again.

I know there are angels walking among us. One of them was there that evening with my sister!

One day while at home from the hospital and washing my car, young Randy walked toward me with a puzzled look on his face after getting off the school bus. He was looking around, so I asked him what he was doing. He told me that he had seen someone standing behind me. There was no one there but me… at least, not that I could see! I think the angels were there to prepare me for what was to come.

> *Your ears will hear a voice behind you, saying, "This is the way; walk in it."*
> ISAIAH 30:21 (NIV)

We are all so very blessed.

Michael had made it through another hurdle. I felt blessed because I had received the answer to my prayers. I feel blessed and thankful for a wonderful loving and supportive family.

Although every family member recalled feeling as though this disease was like a roller coaster ride, at that moment I felt that we could handle anything.

Michael attempted to start college again. Before long, it was time to be tested to see if he was still in remission.

6

On September 11, 2001, a day that will forever be a part of history, Michael was lying on a bed in the clinic getting ready for his spinal tap. It was just another ordinary day for us. Then, I heard some commotion in the hall, so I went to see what was happening. The nurses and doctors were crowded into one small room in front of the television. I could not believe what I was seeing! A plane had struck one of the World Trade Towers in New York City! As with every person in the country and around the world, we were all in shock and did not know what to make of it. Then, another broadcast came on the television. A second plane had struck the Pentagon in Washington, DC. Then another crashed into the other tower of the World Trade Center. Everyone was in a state of shock, and I started questioning whether it was a good idea to sedate Michael with our country being under attack. The doctors decided it would be in Michael's best interest to go ahead with the procedure.

Now, when people are talking and remembering where and what they were doing on that day, I think back and remember that it was the most horrific day for all of America. My son Michael, at the age of twenty-one, relapsed that day for the second time. I cannot even begin to describe the despair I felt.

The doctor informed us that Michael had received the lifetime limit on some of the drugs used in his chemo treatment. Apparently, some drugs used in various chemotherapy regimens have a lifetime limit due to their cumulative toxic effect. These drugs have a risk of cardiac toxicity and can cause congestive heart failure. They could do nothing further for him, except make him comfortable when his final days approached.

The only way I can explain how I felt at that moment is to say that I felt as if someone had cut off my air supply. I simply could not breathe.

Michael's doctor suggested that we go to Duke University Hospital in Durham, North Carolina, to discuss a cord blood transplant.

After a baby is born, the blood is harvested from the umbilical cord. It does no harm to the baby in any way. Like bone marrow, cord blood is unique because it contains a very large number of healthy stem cells, and this type of treatment offered the best and final chance for a cure of Michael's disease.

Donating cord blood helps to save lives. Sometimes parents of a newborn store the umbilical cord, in the event someone in their family may need it. Unfortunately, umbilical cords are frequently discarded. Cord blood stem cells are not embryonic stem cells and are not controversial. Nevertheless, they have the power to save and change lives!

We returned home from Charlottesville, Virginia, after receiving the news of the relapse. Michael was so emotionally torn that he left the house and did not return for a few hours. Our families came to be with us. It was late, and the whole family was distraught.

My husband Randy explained that he felt confused in his feelings most of the time, not really knowing how to deal with the constantly changing news about Michael. Over time, he couldn't help but wonder how much more hurt we would all be able to take, not knowing what was going to happen from one day to the next. I did not have the answer to his question, "When will this be over?"

I could feel the tension building between us. We were forced to be apart, and our family unit was in trouble. I knew that he was worried about Michael, and that he felt set aside and forgotten because my focus was always on Michael. He just wanted it to be over, so that he would not have to think about it again. Our marriage was strained, and we were discussing divorce. This illness was threatening our whole family.

Michael and I stayed up late talking about everything, and crying. He said, "Mom... I don't think I can go through this anymore."

How was I to convince him not to give up? I just wasn't ready to let go of him. I told him that if he did this, that there was a chance that it would make him feel sick and that it might not even work at all. But there was a chance.

"It could work and make you well again, you cannot give up!" I said to him.

This is why I chose to have WNTGVUP on my license plate. It stands for, 'won't give up'.

"We can never give up! Never lose our faith and our hope."

May the God of hope fill you with all joy and peace as you trust in him, so that you may overflow with hope by the power of the Holy Spirit.

ROMANS 15:13 (NIV)

I was finally so exhausted from talking and crying that I went to bed but could not really get to sleep. I lay there and prayed, "God, give me strength to handle yet another hurdle."

I did not want to give up on Michael, but I knew it was out of my hands.

The next morning, Michael gave me a poem he had written that night after our talk. It read as follows:

When you close your eyes you see darkness.
When I close my eyes, I feel tired and sorrow.
These eyes are not your eyes to see with.
When you look up you see the sky.
When I look up, I see the Heavens extending a
helping hand to me and telling me to stay around
for a while longer.
I can see the seconds echoing as the minutes pass
by one by one, while you can only hear them.
You see the world as it is.
I see the world like it is turning inside out.
How do you know how it feels to be me?
Have you ever walked my line in my shoes?
Are you willing to bend to the point of breaking?
How can you tell me it will be fine and I'll be ok?
Have you ever felt like your body was consuming itself?
I often feel like a bull without horns.
I can't win the fight against time.
Just as I'm ready to give in,
I see that look in your eyes.
For you it is worth the fight…. Always."

We had our Thanksgiving dinner together as a family. We even set a place for Michael's little dog, Amber. She wore a white napkin around her neck, and we all enjoyed our dinner. I expect she enjoyed it the most! As for the rest of us that day, it was not only the food we were thankful for... we were thankful for so much more. We were all together as a family. Even though this was one of the most difficult times of our lives, we were able to share good food and laughter and just be together.

God had heard my prayers again. Michael had decided to make the trip to Duke and not give up. I thank God every day for my boys, my husband, family and friends. I try very hard not to take them for granted. I tell them every time I talk to them that I love them. I do this with all of my family, so that if there is ever a time they are no longer with me, or I with them, there will not be any doubt how much we loved one another. We can live without any regrets about this. So many people wonder, in similar circumstances, "Did I do enough? Did they know how much I loved them?" Do not leave it to chance. Tell them everyday.

We left for Duke University after Thanksgiving to discuss the procedure, and to meet the doctors who were going to be caring for him. Michael was still not sure about the whole thing, until he talked with the doctor who would be in charge of his treatment. This man was so kind, and even though there were risks involved, he put most of our fears to rest. Michael felt good about him right away and wanted to begin as soon as possible.

We went home with mixed, but many positive, feelings.

Maybe this will work.

I had some things to wrap up before we left, and I went for my annual checkup. The test found something on my ovary. Oh great, I thought, now what!

The doctor said that I should have surgery as soon as possible. There was no way that I could do this! The only thing I could think of then was getting Michael to Duke for his transplant.

I did the only thing I could do at the time... I put it off.

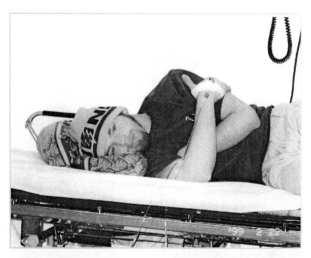

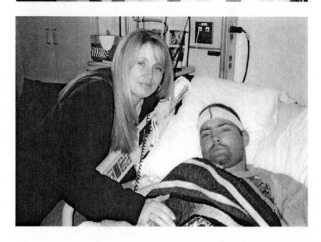

7

I had always been so concerned with Michael that I overlooked how devastating it was for Michael's brother, Randy. He never really talked much about it, but I saw his grades drop and he was withdrawn. When I think of all the times he was awakened in the middle of the night and still expected to concentrate in school, I find myself wondering how all of this has deeply affected him.

We had to leave. There were no words to tell him how emotionally torn I felt. I knew that I had to be with Michael, but Randy was in so much pain that it broke my heart to leave him. Looking back, I wish I had taken him along with me.

Every single part of this horrible disease is hard to go through, but I overlooked one of the most important aspects. I have learned from this entire experience that cancer affects the whole family. It primarily affects the one who has it, but also the rest of the family who love that person.

I have never seen my husband cry so hard and so much. Although Randy is Michael's stepfather and they have not always seen eye to eye, I knew that he loved Michael. Although he never said so, I realized now just how much Michael's illness really affected him. It was a goodbye in which neither of them knew if they would ever see each other again because of the risks involved.

On January 1, 2002, we left for Duke with all of our hopes and fears, wondering if this was the end of his journey or the beginning of a completely new life. Everything was dependent upon the success of the transplant and if his body would accept the new cells. It was a risky procedure, but we had run out of options.

On the drive there, Michael and I did not know quite what to say to each other. There was a silence in the car because I knew I had to have a discussion with him that no parent should ever have to have with his or her child. We had to talk about life support and Michael's final wishes, should something go wrong. Michael said that he did not want a machine keeping him alive, and that he did not want to be placed on life support. I prayed, "Oh God, guide me to do the right thing and give Michael the strength to survive this."

We arrived in Durham, North Carolina, the night a snowstorm hit, and checked into the hotel to get ready for the busy day ahead of us. Everyone we talked to said that the town usually did not get that kind of snow!

Michael had to go through total body radiation for a week. Surprisingly, his body took it well, and he did not have any burns. However, we were not sure what side effects it was going to bring in the future. Nevertheless, he had to have it to kill off any cancer cells that might be hiding.

He was admitted to the hospital so that they could begin bringing his immune system down in order to give the new cord blood the best chance of being successful. Instead of just the one unit of cord blood, he was to receive three units from three different cords. This was experimental, and partially because Michael was older and bigger, he was going to require more for his body weight. His body would have a greater chance of accepting one of three units.

We were on the fifth floor of the hospital. Passing through one set of doors, lockers lined one wall. The other wall had sinks where we had to wash and sterilize our hands before pressing a buzzer for permission to enter a second set of doors. To the right, and all the way down the hall, we arrived at room number 5208 in the corner of a suite of sixteen rooms with other seriously ill children. I became attached to those children and their parents in the six-plus months that we were there.

When we settled in, the nurses invited us to the patient lounge for a young teenager's birthday party. She was very quiet and reserved. She had lost all of her hair. There were party hats and favors for everyone. For a moment, there was laughter, and then everyone went back to his or her room.

Pictures hung outside each room of every child and their families. Some of the families had to sell everything they had to save their child's life. One family sold a farm that had been in the family for generations.

Although it was a tough time for the children and their families, the doctors and nurses tried to keep everyone's spirits up. There were games and movies. Outside each room there was a table that folded down for the nurses to write on. We covered them with sheets, and armed the kids with squirt guns filled with sterile water. They loved to soak the nurses. It was so wonderful to see smiles on the faces of those sick children, to see them escape the reality of their illness for at least a while.

Not long after the birthday party, I stepped into the hall and felt an uneasy feeling come over me. I saw a lot of doctors and nurses at room of the young birthday girl. People were crying, and the nurse was leading her parents to another room, the room that everyone would come to dread. We lost her that day. I say "we" because everyone on that floor became a part of us. We were all there for each other, and for the same reason... to save our child's life.

I went back into Michael's room upset. Michael did not want

me to become attached to the kids because he saw how emotionally
draining it was for me. He was being protective of me, as always.
However, it was impossible. You could not be on that floor and not
be humbled by all of those children. I fell in love with all of them.

Sadly, we lost five children on that floor within the first two
months. And there was always someone else waiting to fill their
rooms.

Before Michael's diagnosis, I was not aware that there were so
many children with this sickness, and so many families struggling to
find a way to come up with the money for treatment.

Michael had many people's prayers. All of our family and friends
prayed for him. He was on prayer chains across the country. He
received a lot of cards with well wishes, even from people he did not
even know. An elementary school class sent a big envelope full of
cards that the kids had made for him. Michael said he was amazed
at the number of people who cared for him. I laid the cards across

him in the bed and took a picture. Such an outpouring of compassion from total strangers restores your faith in humanity.

Love is powerful and an amazing feeling!

Beloved, if God so loved us, we also ought to love one another.
   1 John 4:11

I was particularly fond of one little seven year old girl named Elizabeth. She was very shy at first, but her mom told me she really liked Michael and me. I think she actually had a crush on Michael! She usually didn't take to people that fast. I recall a time when the kids all had squirt guns and she was just soaking everyone who passed by her room, but when I walked by she had that shy little smile on her face and let me pass without squirting me!

Elizabeth's birthday was coming up, so I went to the store to purchase all the fresh ingredients needed for her cake and I made sure it was the freshest it could be. I returned to the apartment that

I was renting in the area to bake it. She was so happy. I really came to love that little girl!

During our stay there, we were introduced to the Best Buddy Program. Michael was assigned a friend from the program, who came to talk with him and play games or just to watch a movie. The program allowed the parents to take a breather, or to run errands. Not that we wanted to be away from our children. It just allowed us to recharge and be better at coping with things.

My favorite places to go were the gardens, and the amazing chapel with its beautiful wooden pews, tall arched ceilings, and stained glass windows. Once, when I went to the chapel, a man with a violin walked up to the front and started playing, as if he were playing for Jesus. It echoed throughout the tall ceilings and off the pews. Such heavenly music! It allowed me a little time to breathe. I was extremely grateful for The Buddy Program.

Michael's buddy even stayed with him while I had the surgery that I had to put off before we left. I tried to go back to Michael's room the night of my surgery, but the nurses said that I was as pale as a ghost. My husband came to take care of me. Fortunately, I was able to recoup at the apartment for a day.

Michael's buddy also surprised all of us by giving Michael a gift certificate for his birthday! Only, it was to go skydiving! Michael had told him it was something he had always wanted to do. I don't think his doctors thought much of the idea. In addition, the agreement was that if something were to happen to Michael, that I would have to promise to jump instead! Now, I am terrified of heights, but I reluctantly agreed to do this for Michael.

The coordinators of the Buddy program once approached me about speaking to a group of people who were trying to decide if the Buddy program would be right for them. My first thought was that I couldn't do it, since I was never comfortable talking in front of a group of people. I had always been a shy person growing up. However, I knew what a difference this program made to the lives of the parents and their children on the floor, so I agreed.

I was very nervous when I walked into the conference room and saw the long table with people looking at me. I thought that my throat was going to close up! After I introduced myself – I don't know how to explain what came over me – everything just started pouring out effortlessly. I told them Michael's story. Then I told them how I had to be there with him by myself since my husband Randy had to stay at home to continue working and take care of our younger son, Randy. I explained to them how it became overwhelming at times for some of the parents. Some didn't even have a vehicle for transportation to the store for food and necessities. This was where the Buddy program helped, I said. If caregivers could catch a break for just thirty minutes, it is a blessing.

By the time I was finished talking, there was not a dry eye in the room.

From that day on, I talk to everyone to share our story.

The woman in charge of putting the meeting together told me later that everyone in the room had volunteered for the "Best Buddy Program" that day! It was such a good feeling to be able to help the families on that floor.

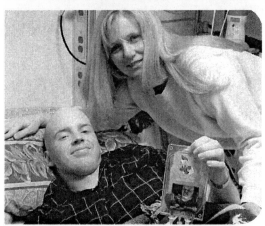

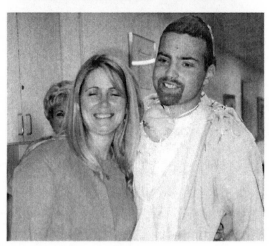

8

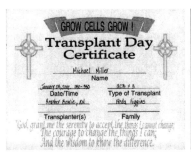

On January 23, they hung the first of three bags of cord blood, which looked like watered down Kool-Aid. The donors of all three units were female. So a male nurse who liked giving Michael a hard time brought him issues of Martha Stewart and Better Homes magazines!

"Oh, that's hilarious," said Michael!

All of the nurses were amazing. I cannot say enough about everyone we met on that floor.

After receiving the cord blood, the room gave off an odor of creamed corn! That was weird, the whole room smelled like corn!

Cord blood transplants are administered through a central line or IV. Many people I spoke with thought it was a surgical procedure and more complicated. All went well that day. The nurse hung a transplant certificate outside of Michael's door that said, "Grow, Cells, Grow!"

There were toys in the hall for all of the kids, and a tricycle that Michael later managed to squeeze himself onto. He peddled down the hallway as fast as he could. He had everyone in tears from laughing so hard. It was hard for anyone not to fall in love with him.

I slept in a cot in the corner of Michael's room. Michael kept his room at a low temperature, so I was always freezing! Even the nurses wore sweaters in his room.

Michael hung posters of his Maryland Basketball team on the wall, along with his jersey. One day, the door to his room opened quickly and his nurse told him that the Duke Basketball players were on their way in to visit the patients, and that he should probably take his stuff down so they would not be offended!

Michael said "No way!"

We thought that he was not excited about the visit, but what he really meant was that he would not take his team poster down for them!

This was the year that Duke and Maryland were in the NCAA Championship. When players entered his room they tried to give him a hard time about his team, but Michael gave it right back to them!

Before the players left the room, they all told Michael they had great admiration for him for standing up and believing in his Maryland team. They also tried to get a last dig in by wishing his team luck in the championship.As they were walking out, Michael said, "No, good luck to you, because you're going to need it!"

They all got a big kick out of that, and went out the door laughing!

Maryland won the championship that year!

It was wonderful having these young men taking time to visit all the children on that floor.

A comedian also came to the floor for a visit. It was Jeff Foxworthy. What a treat! When I told him that I was Michael's mom, he said that I should be telling everyone that I was his sister instead! He stayed and talked awhile, and we got him to autograph a picture for my brother, Mike, who was a big fan of Jeff's. Jeff wrote "You might be a redneck if your name is Uncle Mike!"

This man was so comfortable to be around, we didn't even think to get our picture taken with him! What was I thinking? He was also the Honorary Chairman of the Duke Children's Classic Golf Tournament to raise money for the hospital. What an extraordinary man to take time from his busy schedule to do this and just visit the kids!

NASCAR fans on the floor also received a visit from the drivers!

On the second day of his treatment, Michael started having stomach pains. He was not able to eat much that day. On the third day, he felt much better and was able to eat French toast! Michael felt good and was able to eat until the seventh day. Then, he stopped eating as much, developed leg pains and a headache. The doctors then put him on high blood pressure medicine.

On the eighth day, Michael's platelets were down, so he received them that night. Because of his allergic reaction

to platelets, he had to be pre-medicated. The platelets gave him hives. He slept all of the next day.

On the ninth day, he was still having severe headaches. He stopped eating, had no appetite, and was unable to taste anything. His temperature rose to one hundred and two degrees.

Finally, he started feeling better. He felt good for several days, so I decided to make a trip back home to see my family. Michael's biological father had come from Florida to stay with him until I returned. It was hard leaving Michael, but it was also very hard to be so far away from my husband and younger son. Before I left the hospital that afternoon to go home, Michael asked me to take care of his dog, Amber. That was all he wanted.

I cried most of the way home... again! The trip was four hours long. When I returned home, I sat in our driveway, mentally and physically exhausted. My husband Randy, came out to greet me, but it was not totally the 'happy-to-see-me' kind of greeting. He said that he had bad news.

I looked up at him with tears running down my face and said, "What, what else could there be?"

"It's Amber," he said. "She got out and was hit by a car. I'm so sorry. She died."

I was in a state of shock. Why? Why was this happening? Especially after Michael had just asked me to take care of her. Now, how in the world was I going to tell him this awful news?

When I returned to the hospital, I did not want to tell him. I was so afraid. I tossed and turned at night agonizing if I should even tell him at all. All of the nurses could tell that there was something wrong. Michael could probably also sense it.

I talked to the counselor about it, and she gave me some very good advice that I still go by today: If you are keeping something to yourself and it does not feel good in your gut, you must tell that person.

So, I got up the courage to tell him.

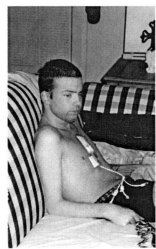

Michael remembers the day we left home to go to Duke University Hospital for the transplant, and he was saying goodbye to Amber. She was looking straight into his eyes and turning her head with watery eyes as if she really knew exactly what was happening. Animals can sense things that are upsetting us.

I don't think he believed me when I first told him what happened to Amber. He said, "No way, that can't be!" He did not cry then, but I could tell he was in shock and devastated. He cried later that night.

Michael also had GVHD, which is the abbreviation for Graph vs. Host Disease. It is the most common and life threatening side effect of a nonrelated stem-cell transplant. HLA matching is the criteria used to determine donor and recipient compatibility and generally refers to six proteins called human leukocyte antigens (HLA) that appear on the surface of white blood cells and other tissues in the body. The transplant can only be performed if there is an adequate HLA match between donor and recipient. A perfect six out of six match is best. Michael's was five out of six. GVHD occurs when the transplanted stem cells from a donor recognize the recipient's body as foreign and then attack it.

Michael turned blistery red. It became uncomfortable to be in his skin. I had to keep an ointment on him, but even that was uncomfortable. However, it could have been much worse had the HLA matching been lower than five out of six!

On the sixteenth day, he started passing blood clots in his urine. The next morning, he felt somewhat better, but it hurt to urinate. After that, he had a tremendous amount of blood in his urine. He was passing blood clots the size of an egg. The nurse was shocked to know that could even happen!

On the nineteenth day after transplant, he contracted an Adenovirus. They started him on a platelet drip.

Adenovirus is a common respiratory infection and urinary tract infection. The virus actually can cause pink eye in healthy people.

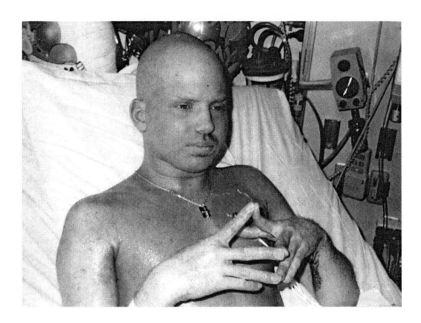

Adenovirus often affects the airway. There are few treatments for this virus, so it is extremely dangerous for the immune-compromised.

Michael became sick to his stomach so often that he didn't have anything left in it. He even named his pail "Ralph." He drew a face in the bottom of it to keep his sense of humor. He would vomit so violently his body would pull the liquid out of his bowel.

It was hard to see him like that, and even harder when he would look up at me to say, "I'm sorry, mom. I'm sorry you have to go through all of this."

Can you believe it? He's thinking about me, as if I was the one going through this. That's just what kind of person Michael is.

The doctors then decided to try Michael on an experimental drug to get the viral infection under control. Michael was actually the first on the floor to receive the drug. But a serious side effect is that it harms the kidneys. Therefore, he had to take another drug to protect them. His stomach was so weak at this point and he was steadily getting worse because he could not hold anything down. He reached the point that when he even saw them bringing the pills he would get sick to his stomach!

Michael began having trouble breathing, so they placed him in a ventilation tent to help him breathe. All of the doctors and nurses had a worried look on their faces.

One nurse even tried to give him a breathing treatment. Michael jerked the mask off his face and raised his voice at her. "I can do it myself!" he said, as he struggled for a breath.

She just walked out of the room, because she knew it was not like him to snap so abruptly. When she returned, Michael apologized to her. She just called him "Darlin'," as she always did and said, "I know all of this is hard for you, and I know you didn't mean anything by it."

Michael was also on drugs for pain, and he was hallucinating. He thought wild dogs were in his room, and that one had bitten him. He wanted to show me where, so he reached for my finger. I thought he was going to point to it, but instead he tried to bite me! He was a very sick boy.

9

Then it happened—the walk to the room where I had seen so many parents go before losing their child. His doctor said that they were moving him to ICU and that it did not look good. They became concerned that the virus was going to attack his heart.

The team of doctors was giving him forty-eight hours before deciding there was nothing further they could do. We talked about Michael's wishes and life support. Even though Michael did not want life support, I asked the doctor if there was even a slight chance he could survive this and he replied, "Michael is very sick and this is life threatening, but of course there is always a slight chance."

Eventually, the doctor had me call all the family. When kids go to the Intensive Care Unit in a condition as bad as Michael's, they generally never come back. However, I heard the doctor say that there was a chance!

I called our family anyway to tell them that we were in danger of losing Michael. Everyone came. I called Michael's dad Jerry from Florida, and he was able to catch a flight to be there. Lifelong friends were there by our side. Everyone who was able to come was there.

The whole family was so distraught. It seemed like Michael's journey was ending.

As they rolled Michael down the hall in his bed, he and I held hands. We told each other how much we loved one another. Even though he had to struggle to take a breath, he told me to do what I thought was best for him. He was having such a difficult time breathing. I was so scared at this point that I could feel my body trembling.

By the time everyone arrived, Michael was already on a ventilator. We had met one of the fathers on the floor who had a beautiful voice and who played the guitar. He went to the Intensive Care Unit where Michael was to sing for him. As he was singing "Breathe" by Michael W. Smith, I was standing over Michael praying. When he got to the lyrics that said, "I'm desperate for you," "I'm lost without you," tears were streaming down my face, soaking Michael's gown. I felt His presence in that room.

That night, Michael's dad, Jerry, my husband, Randy, and I were in the room, and I was holding Michael's hand, rubbing it with no response from him. It was hard looking at him and not being able to see those beautiful green eyes, and the thought of never hearing his voice again had become overwhelming. I felt that I would collapse.

My husband and I went back to the apartment to get everyone settled. The next morning I walked into the room and Michael's head looked distorted. He had developed a pressure wound or 'decubitus ulcer' from his head being in one position for too long. The pressure against the skin reduces blood supply to that area, and the affected tissue dies.

His condition was rapidly deteriorating.

All of our family took their turn going in to stay with Michael and to say their goodbyes. Betty and Louie had to say goodbye to the boy who had become their grandson. It was hard to see them all so upset. My brother and his wife Annette said that it took the wind out of them.

My sister stood outside the glass looking at Michael hooked up to the machines that were keeping him alive. Michael looked so tired and weak. To help her with the torn feelings of what was best for Michael and what she had wanted for him all these years, Nancy looked for the angel she had previously seen in the Charlottesville Intensive Care Unit. Then, she and our brother went to the garden area, crying and praying for Michael.

I remember taking my dad in to see Michael. In all of my years growing up, I have never seen or heard my father like that before. I had never heard my father talk to God! He was pleading with God to let it be him instead in that bed. "Oh Michael," he cried, "It shouldn't be you lying there, honey. I love you, Michael."

Then, it was time to take Randy to see his brother. Randy looked at his brother on a ventilator hooked up to machines with multiple lines, and seemed devastated at the thought of never seeing Michael again. He began to cry.

I have since learned that the pain that a sibling feels should never be taken lightly. Randy explained how he had missed his brother so much, and that he just wanted him back, and for things to return to normal.

Later, Randy told me that he had been living in a fantasy telling himself that Michael would be all right, when deep down he felt that it would never be the same for Michael again. He said that when Michael and I left for Duke for the cord blood transplant that his days grew cold, and that he was in a very dark place. Sadness, depression and many other feelings had overwhelmed him. Even so, he kept it all inside.

Unfortunately, those feelings turned into something far worse when he and his father received the call that Michael might not make it. He remembers being so angry and blaming God when he did not have the answer as to why this was happening to his brother. He was certain that God was taking his best friend, his brother, away from him. He had come to the decision that he was not going to live without him. Although he had never mentioned this to anyone, he was prepared to go with Michael.

I knew that all of this was having a devastating impact on him, but I did not think for one moment he would be thinking of taking his own life!

This was one of the hardest confessions to hear from a child. I had felt guilty that I had to leave him for such long periods of time to be with Michael. I wanted so desperately to save one child's life. Even though I had prayed to God to be with Randy every night and to be there to comfort him and keep him safe while I was gone, I had placed him in jeopardy.

He told me that somewhere along the way he had developed different feelings of concern for me as his mom. He said that I stood out further than anyone else did, and that he knew I felt his pain as he felt mine. Therefore, if this were to be the end of Michael's journey, he was glad to be there for his family and me. The love in my heart and my prayers for my children were answered. God had kept him safe.

Randy Mathew also believed that the true point was to stick together no matter what, and never give up on the ones who would never give up on you. I am so proud of the man he has become, a gentle, caring, loving soul.

It broke my heart to see him cry like that, so I decided to lighten it up by telling him about Michael's prank phone calls. Randy wiped away the tears and looked at me with a puzzled look on his face. His facial expression dropped! He said, "You mean to tell me, that was him all of those months!" He hung his head. Then he looked up with a grin, wiping his eyes, and said, "See, that's what made it fun! I love being his brother."

I walked Randy Mathew back to the waiting area where the rest of our family was waiting.

I felt a great urgency to head to the Chapel on the Duke grounds. I sat in one of the back rows and began to pray. I have always prayed for the strength to make it through things, but this time was different. I prayed as I have never prayed before. I asked the Lord for a miracle.

> *Whatever we ask, we receive of Him, because we keep his commandments and do those things that are pleasing in His sight.*
>
> 1 JOHN 3:22

I pleaded with Him "Please help the doctors save Michael. I don't want to give him up, but whatever happens, I know You will be with him every step of the way. I put my faith in Jesus."

At that moment, I turned Michael over to the Lord, for God knew I could no longer handle this. I sat there for what seemed an eternity with my head hanging down. On my walk back to the hospital, I felt calm, and I had stopped crying.

When I walked into the family waiting area, the look on everyone's face was one of relief! The doctor had a smile on his face as he updated everyone. I will never forget the look on my brother's face. It was not one of despair but of hope and with tears of joy.

Michael's condition had turned for the better. His doctor said he could not begin to explain it, but that they had help on this one.

Wow! What beautiful words coming from a doctor.

When Michael was lying in ICU, seemingly unconscious, with his limp hand in mine, he apparently could still hear us talking. He told me later that when he heard that I was going to leave, he had tried holding onto my hand as tight as he could. But I hadn't felt any movement of his hand. Although he recalls trying to tell me not to go, all I experienced was him just lying there in silence.

Based on this whole ordeal, our perspective on life support systems has changed completely. Now Michael leaves it up to me, and I turn it over to God. I believe that you should never give up on faith or hope. Everything else is out of our hands.

The doctors tried taking him off the ventilator several times before they had success. They even talked of performing a tracheotomy at one point. Michael remembers the nurses taking him off the ventilator. My sister, Nancy, and I were there. I had told him he looked like Rip Van Winkle! I gave him a mirror so that he could see his uni-brow. It went straight across his forehead!

"You had me worried." I said to Michael. "I thought I was going to have to jump from a plane as I had promised your Best Buddy I would!"

It was so good to hear him laugh.

When Michael was finally out of ICU, the nurses on the floor called him a miracle. Even the nurses in that unit told us that they have never seen anyone come back from being in such poor condition.

Hope had been constant in our family and all of the families who prayed for Michael. We may not know the purpose or reason behind all that has come our way, but in time it is revealed to us.

When I start being my human self and feeling sad and angry that this is happening to Michael, I always think of the pain Mary must have felt when Jesus was crucified.

I definitely believe in the power of prayer, especially a mother's prayer for her child, and that our Lord will always do the right thing, even if we don't understand. My brother says he believes in miracles. Some you just have to look for, because they are there.

Michael still had a long road ahead to recovery. He was placed on dialysis because his kidneys were damaged. The doctor placed a temporary access for dialysis in the side of his neck and it was very uncomfortable for Michael with it hanging to the side and pulling downward.

To alleviate his discomfort, I got the idea to use some of the supplies in the room. There was a roll of stretchy material used for dressing wounds, so I used it to make him a headband. Then, just for fun, the nurses and I made him a muscle shirt out of it! He sure did get some laughs out of that one! One nurse even put a third eye on it! She was so much fun! They named me "Nurse of the Month" on their board outside the nurse's station because I helped so much!

Michael's pressure wound had gone almost to his skull. That was one of the most horrible things I had ever seen! Michael recalls being alone in his room and feeling the bandage on his head. He peeled back the dressing to feel why it was there. It felt like a pocket of mush to him. He brought his hand down with blood all over it and called the nurse. The nurses were uncomfortable changing the bandage. The nurse called a wound specialist to teach me how to clean and dress pressure wounds. Every time I took the bandage off, it would take the top layer of the wound off with it. The specialist said Michael was lucky it did not go down to his skull because that takes much longer to heal, if it ever does at all.

When the nurses got Michael settled in his room again, I went out to talk with the doctors. My husband stayed in the room with him. Michael later told me Randy was standing off to the back of him, and he felt him rubbing his head but not saying anything. He said it felt different in the room and he turned to look at him. Tears were running down Randy's face, and he told Michael that he really loved him. Oh my, it probably was a good thing that happened while I was out of the room! I think I have cried enough!

I often wonder if one of the reasons that life-threatening illnesses happen is to bring love into people's lives, to make us all care just a little more about one another. After all, isn't that the greatest gift God has given us?

May the Lord make your love increase and overflow for each other and for everyone else, just as ours does for you.

1 THESSALONIANS 3:12 (NIV)

The love we all have for one another has prevailed, in spite of the many mixed emotions that Michael's illness provoked. I know it brought everyone in our family together. We all put aside our differences. It is an amazing feeling when that occurs. It also brought Michael and his father in Florida closer to each other than ever before. After his father Jerry and I divorced, I had tried to keep them close, but in time his father moved away and we both remarried. After that, he did not see Michael very often. However, with Michael's illness, all of that changed. They both talk and visit more than ever before.

After we were back on the floor, I heard about the little girl Elizabeth I had spoken about earlier. She was not feeling well. She had painted me a picture in her room and her mother brought it to me. Elizabeth was not doing well at all. Due to all of her complications, she had gone into a coma. Her parents knew that I was fond of her. It was no surprise, then, when the doctors asked me to come to her room in the ICU. There was nothing they could do for her. She had been placed on life support.

Her family had the difficult decision to take her off life support. In her case it was the only decision they could make, because she was hemorrhaging internally. They asked me if I wanted to be there to say goodbye. I did not think I could do it, but I knew I had to, for her family and for the little girl I had come to love.

Even now, there is not a day that goes by that I don't think of her. She had given Michael a little blue angel bear and said that it was his guardian angel. It still hangs in my home.

Years have gone by, and we have lost touch with many of the parents from the Duke Hospital. I guess in a way I was trying to forget all of the sadness and move on with my own life. Yet, I have come to learn that I cannot forget. Every time I look at my Michael, I am reminded of how blessed I am, so I need to remember every one of those children and their families. I truly believe that we were brought together on that floor in the hospital at that point in our lives for a reason. We just don't know the full extent of it yet. And I believe we will all be reunited again.

10

Gradually, Michael got some of his strength back. He had to exercise his legs every day to regain the muscle mass that he had lost. I was concerned that he would be unable to climb the stairs to the apartment.

At one point, the nurse had told him not to get out of bed because he would not even be able to stand up on his own. He had to learn to stand and walk all over again. He had so many meds running at one time he named his med pump pole "Sherman the Tank." It was the widest one on the floor! We had to turn it sideways to pass anyone coming down the hall.

Michael became friends with a boy named Joshua. He was younger than Michael, but they were able to talk and joke around. I would wheel Michael down the hall to Joshua's room late at night so that he could write something on his door before morning. Josh would sneak down to Michael's door and write something back! It was usually about their basketball teams. He is the only child of some of the sweetest people I will ever meet. His mother, Sherry, is soft-spoken and his father, Donnie, reminded me of my only brother, whom I missed back home. He actually looked a lot like him! When

I told him he reminded me of my brother, he started calling me "Sis". On Valentine's Day, Donnie and Sherry brought spaghetti dinner for everyone on the floor! What wonderful people!

Eventually, they too, lost their beautiful child, Joshua. Even with this devastating loss, their hearts remained filled with love for others. I still talk to them, and they have even taken their vacation time to come and visit Michael.

The hospital finally released Michael in the following month.

Everyone threw a big party in the hallway. I had bought silly string for all of the kids.

The male nurse who always teased Michael now looked like a creature from another planet when they were finished spraying him. I remember feeling happy about taking Michael to the apartment, but frightened I would not be able to take care of him and keep him safe.

I was responsible for giving him his meds on time and there were a lot of them, including TPN (overnight nutrition through IV), and making sure everything was germ-free. I had to change the dressing on his central line going into his chest and the pressure wound on his head. However, I just did what I had to do at the time, and we got through it somehow.

We returned to the clinic for routine visits for blood work and lab tests. There were many trips to the ER for high fevers and regular trips for dialysis. It was hard for Michael to gain weight because not only was he on dialysis, he was diabetic.

He couldn't eat any of his favorite foods anymore. His weight was steadily going down, and the doctors were concerned. Michael had gone from 138lbs. to 117lbs. in less than two weeks, so back to the hospital he went.

Finally, at the end of June, the doctors were ready to release Michael to go home. After six months, we were really going home!

11

Before Michael left the hospital, my husband came a few days early. Michael had talked about wanting another dog, but the doctors advised us not to have any pets. I had made up my mind though, Michael had already missed so much of his life, and he was missing his dog, Amber.

So, a few days before he was released, my husband and I went on a search for a dog for Michael!

We found a breeder who had Great Dane puppies. We picked the one that was sitting in the corner. He too looked like he needed a friend because he was sitting all by himself. He was white, peppered with black splotches all over him. The day that the doctor released Michael, we loaded up the car and put the pup in the back seat. I went in to get Michael while my husband stayed in the car. I could not wait to see his face!

We loaded all of his things into the trunk of the car and Michael was holding his pillow. He opened the door to throw the pillow in. The look on his face was priceless! There sat a brand new puppy looking up at him, someone to start the next chapter of his life with.

"Marley" was the name Michael picked out for him. Michael loved Bob Marley's music, which always had a calming effect on him, so we thought it was the perfect name for a companion.

Michael always says that Marley played an important roll in his recovery. I suppose I took a major risk by bringing a dog into our home, but I saw how that dog got him through some very tough months, and how much they loved one another. If there was a chance it could bring some joy to his life, it was worth it. We just had to take precautions. Marley could not sleep with Michael and absolutely no kisses in the face! Washing hands was necessary (as it always should be!)

We settled back into our home.

The doctor admitted Michael to UVA Hospital in Charlottesville, Virginia, on June 8, 2002, because he had a glucose reading of over one thousand and it is not supposed to be over one hundred! The doctors were amazed he was even sitting up and able to talk.

A group of students came in with a doctor, but they soon left because he said this was out of the norm and he just didn't have an explanation for them! The doctors were able to bring his glucose levels back down slowly and they released him without any complications.

We heard Duke was having a fundraiser for the children's floor, so my sister-in-law, Annette, and her sister Penny and I raised money and went to the event. Everyone had to walk around the track for the event. Michael was still weak and very thin, but he was determined to make the walk. His doctors and some of his nurses were there, and they could not believe that he was doing this. He held a balloon and wrote Joshua's name on it in memory of the friend we lost, and he wore a shirt that read "I took a step for a hero."

We had to hold Michael up part of the way, but he did it! He did it for Joshua and for all of the other children. At the end of the walk, everyone gathered and released the balloons as they played "Some-

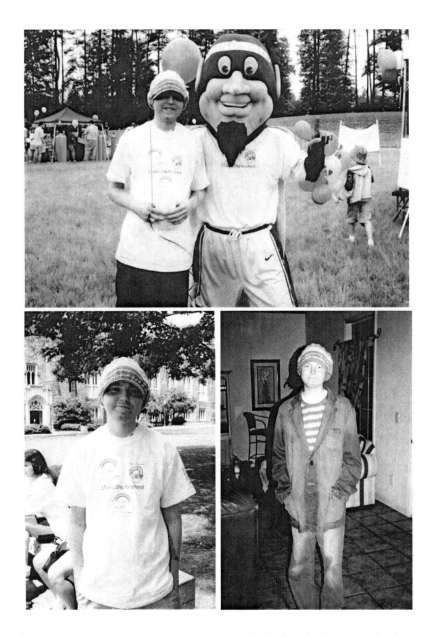

where over the Rainbow" in memory of all the children we had lost. There was not a dry eye that day.

Later, we found out we were one of the top fundraisers! What an awesome feeling to be able to give back to the people who helped save my son and to help the families who were just beginning their journey.

After we went home, Michael became withdrawn and depressed. He started to question why he was still here and why all of those other children were gone. I tried many times to get him to come out of his room. He would just sit in his room by himself. The cord blood transplant was very hard on him. I began to wonder if this was my fault. After all, it was I who made the decision to put Michael on life support.

I questioned if I were just being selfish, but that didn't last long. It was worth having him with me, and alive.

It was time for his two-year check up at Duke. After all of his tests were over, we went to visit the fifth floor to say hello to his doctors and nurses. He had made a painting for them to hang in the unit. It read,

> *"We are living art created to hang on,*
> *Stand up, continue and encourage others.*
> *Hope is an art. Continue to practice it."*

—Maya Angelou

Michael was surprised to find out most of the new people had heard about him, and some even wanted his room! The doctors and nurses were all happy to see him doing so well. They told him that kids like him were the reason they came to work every day.

It is a very stressful job, but if they can save even one life, it is all worth it. If it were not for survivors like Michael, they would not feel like they were doing great work and saving lives. It makes all of the hard work and long stressful hours worth it.

Michael got the answer he had been searching for on that day.

12

February 17, 2003, I took Michael back to the hospital with pancreatitis again. Fortunately, it was a mild case, so the doctor released him on the twenty-fifth of that month. I reluctantly recall another earlier trip to the ER, because we had thought it was his pancreas again. It ended up being a bad case of chili I had fixed for him! The pain was just gas in his stomach! Well.... it took a while for his doctor to stop teasing me about my famous chili. We spent hours in the emergency room because of it!

Then, on March 5th, one day before his birthday, I rushed him in again. He had a fever and had to be hospitalized. His doctor released him the following day, after blood cultures were collected. He felt fine and there was no fever. However, on the 7th at 1:00 a.m., his fever returned. He was shaking, and his temperature had risen to 103.6. His doctor re-admitted him.

Because of bacteria in his blood, the central line had to be removed again. He was discharged on March 14th.

Michael was being dialyzed three times a week at this point.

On March 28th, he was having trouble with his line again. On

April 1st, Michael was admitted for his central line. He was constantly having issues with it. It would clot, or there would be an obstruction further up the artery in his neck. In addition, he had many infections in the line. The doctor placed a graft in his arm for dialysis. He was discharged on April 5th.

He was admitted again on April 7th for a glucose reading of 38, and released on the 9th.

He was admitted again on April 15th. His potassium levels were at 7.7, very dangerous levels for his heart. They also started him on overnight nutrition through his central line. He was still losing weight. He was discharged on April 21st, and I had to hook him up to a pump for his nutrition, like so many times before.

On May 29th, Michael had to have a biopsy of his stomach because he was not gaining weight. His stomach always bothered him. He was admitted again June 12th for a CT scan and MRI. The tests had determined he had influenza. He was treated and released.

This is how our months were spent, in and out of the hospital for different ailments.

On one of the trips when we were having trouble with his central line, we went to angioplasty. There was a blockage in the line. The technicians were able to remove it, but when they were finished, Michael complained that his chest and side were hurting. They thought it might have been a pulled muscle from rolling him over on the table. However, when we made it up to the floor where he was to be dialyzed, it was becoming hard for him to take a breath, and he couldn't even stand up straight. They took x-rays and found out that he had a collapsed lung!

His lung had been punctured when they were trying to remove the clot. A chest tube was placed so he could breathe. Since we had been through so much together, nothing surprised Michael or me any more.

13

Because Michael had been on dialysis for years by this point, he was placed on the kidney transplant list. Michael's dad Jerry was tested and found to be a suitable donor match for a kidney. He went through all of the tests and everything was a go. We just had one problem. We had no place for his dog Marley to stay. I would have to stay with Michael to care for him and my husband worked a lot. So, we had to find another home for Marley and we did! It was with a couple without children who loved dogs and had always wanted a Great Dane. We were heartbroken, but we knew that he was in a safe place with people who loved him.

Michael went back to Duke and we found a place to stay in the area. Then, at the last minute, the organ transplant surgery was canceled because of his dad's age. Michael was disappointed, but did not want any harm to come to his dad. I was tested as a possible alternative.

When I was young, I had some health issues, so I was told by the medical team that I would have to be placed on some medicine before the transplant, and that there was a risk of me going into total liver failure from the drug. Michael was adamant about me not doing it. He did not want anything happening to me. The doctor told him the transplant procedure would probably be available sooner if he went for a kidney and a pancreas transplant.

There are a lot of people waiting for a kidney but fewer for a dual kidney-pancreas transplant. In addition, it would be easier if he got both from the same person. His body wouldn't have to fight against two different donor organs.

Michael was in contact with people working at the Mayo Clinic in Jacksonville, Florida, where many transplants are performed. He was able to get an appointment and they accepted him as a transplant candidate.

To prepare for the procedure, Michael had to have all kinds of tests, so he moved to Florida to be with his dad.

We hoped that he wouldn't have long to wait for the organs, but on the other hand, I felt uncomfortable at times wishing for that. It meant that another person's life would end to give Michael a chance for a somewhat normal life.

2008 was the presidential election year. My husband and I decided we ought to vote with absentee ballots, because we were concerned that we might be called to Florida when Michael had his trasplant.

Michael received a call from the hospital in the middle of a severe storm. They had found a match! Then they called him back to tell him it was a no-go because the storm was so bad that they were unable to get the organs to the hospital.

This was like being on a rollercoaster, and not being able to get off. We had to console ourselves, knowing that at least someone else got the organs.

On the evening of November 3, 2008, we got the call. Michael was going to get his transplant! Off to Florida we went, and drove all night.

Michael was just coming out of surgery when we arrived at the hospital the next morning. We were standing in his room when they wheeled him in. I could not believe it when I saw him! The color had come back in his body. He actually looked good for someone just having had major surgery. Michael had staples from his sternum down to his pelvis. He called it his zipper belly.

He actually had three kidneys and two pancreases inside of him! He said his stomach felt full all of the time!

The nurses had him up walking that very night. Amazing!

His new kidney was putting out a good amount of urine directly after his surgery! His doctors were pleased, and said that it was a good sign.

Michael showed me a piece of paper that he had on his lap in dialysis the day before he got the call. His blood had dropped on it when the nurse was taking him off the dialysis machine and trying to get his arm to clot. Michael said that it was a sign from Jesus that he was going to get his transplant! The blood was in the shape of a cross! He keeps it in his bible.

I believe with all my heart that Michael is still here because God wants him here.

Michael was in the hospital for seven days after his transplant. After he was released, we were only in the apartment for a few days before Michael started getting dehydrated.

Back to the hospital we went.

The doctor admitted him for a few more days. The new kidney had to stay well-hydrated or he could lose it.

While Michael was in the hospital, his dad and I had bought Michael another puppy. She was a brindle boxer from Kentucky.

The breeder drove down to Florida to deliver her to me. When Michael was released from the hospital, he became attached to the puppy right away. Laughter once again filled our temporary home. He decided to name her "Reesie," because her color reminded him of the Reese's peanut butter cup candy. She has the biggest brown eyes, and when you look at her, you can't help but smile! Reesie played a major roll in Michael's recovery from the dual organ transplants. He could not go out much, so she occupied a lot of his time. Animals are a blessing, too!

I stayed through Thanksgiving with Michael and Reesie. He was looking forward to a home-cooked meal for Thanksgiving. We had so much to be thankful for!

Before the transplant, Michael was living in St. Augustine Florida with his grandfather in a condominium owned by Michael's dad. Everything there had to be completely cleaned and sanitized due to Michael's weak immune system. Michael's father had the carpet cleaned along with the air ducts and unit. The doctors told us that dust could be very dangerous for him to breathe.

We made trips to the condominium to take Michael's belongings to the apartment we had rented in Jacksonville. Early one morning, I said goodbye to Michael and headed home after being in Florida for a month.

Michael was able to move back to Virginia after that first year.

Michael is still self-conscious of the graft for dialysis that remains in his arm although it is never accessed. The long-term effects of the radiation have scarred his tear ducts leaving his eyes swollen and tearing most of the time. It has destroyed the pigment in his skin, making it impossible for him to be in the sun for any length of time, and has left his skin with dark and light spots. His hair used to be thick and wavy and now it is much thinner.

Michael says the kidney/pancreas transplant was like a walk in the park compared to the cord blood transplant, which changed so

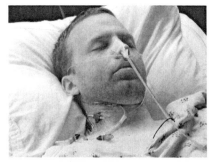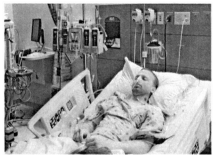

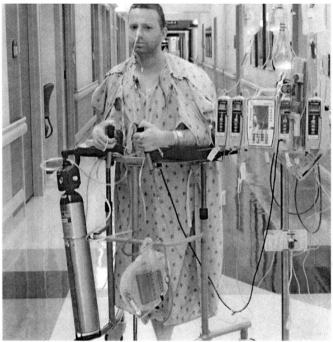

many things he liked about himself. His strong sense of self-confidence has never quite returned.

What I see when I look at him is that same sweet, handsome, kind spirit he has always been: someone who can make me laugh on my worst day. I am so proud of him, and he is my miracle.

Michael still returns occasionally to the University of Virginia Hospital, in Charlottesville, Virginia, to Duke University Hospital, in Durham, North Carolina, and to The Mayo Clinic in Jacksonville,

Florida, to visit the doctors and nurses who all played a roll in saving his life.

At the age of thirty-one, he has started college again. Michael has wanted this for so long. He is thoroughly enjoying it, and has a 4.0 grade average. Reesie is still his faithful companion and my furry grandchild! Happily, Michael is still able to visit Marley, the Great Dane that helped him recover from the cord blood transplant.

We have had a lot of laughs and good times. Michael has stayed the course, and his faith in the Lord has grown strong.

The past now seems so distant, but I will never forget everything we have been through together as a family, and we will never give up.

Then shall your light break forth like the dawn, your healing shall spring up speedily; your righteousness shall go before you; the glory of the Lord shall be your rear guard.

ISAIAH 58:8 (ESV)

Michael made me this Mother's Day card in 2009 after his kidney/pancreas transplant, in which he included the image of his heart-shaped drop of blood. Inside the card was a picture of an empty hospital bed.

HAPPY MOTHERS DAY!

"You have turned my mourning into joyful dancing. You have taken away my cloths of mourning and clothed me with joy that I might sing praises to you and not be silent. O Lord My God, I will give thanks forever!"

PSALMS 30:11-12

This couldn't have been possible without you, Mom. May this bed stay empty many more years to come.

Love you always and forever,

Michael

TESTIMONIALS OF MICHAEL'S
STRENGTH AND COURAGE

"Michael, it is hard to find the words to tell you how precious you are to us. You are a true blessing and God has a plan for you. We love you and will always keep you in our hearts."

—Donnie & Sherry Frost
    Father and Mother of Joshua

"Michael,
You have inspired our family with your amazing and courageous fight for life. So many of us take our lives for granted but you have encouraged us with your strength and hope, to never give up. We now understand why your name is Michael. The first letter of your name stands for miracle - God's miracle. And the last letter stands for Life—enjoy your journey!
    Miracle
    Inspiring
    Courageous
    Hope
    Amazing
    Encouraging
    Life
We love you and know Gods love is with you and all around you."

—Aunt Shelby and Uncle Jack

"Mike is a good friend and a true inspiration. Although he has been through so much, he has maintained a positive attitude and uplifting spirit. He has taught me never to give up, to fight for what you love and everything is possible."

—Brad Parlette
One of Michael's closest childhood friends since elementary school

"First and foremost, Mike is my best friend, he has always been an inspiration in my life, I am truly blessed to know him."

—Mike Quillen
Michael's best friend growing up

"My senior year of high school I was awoken one night by a phone call that changed my life. Receiving the news that my best friend was diagnosed with leukemia immediately changed my teenage notions of immortality. The following day as I walked the halls between class expecting to see Mike and exchange gestures as we were accustomed to, I was reminded of the lesson I had learned the previous night. Perhaps for the first time my concerns were not those of a social or selfish nature. Over the course of the following years there would be many ups and downs and many times I questioned why God would let this happen to my friend who was so much of a better person than I... Like his mother and many who know him I wish I could take the burden from him. Mike went through many physical changes throughout his battle with cancer but his will and spirit remained the same. It was his spirit that strengthened those around him, when we all were trying to be strong for him. Empathizing with his struggle is impossible for me and I would be disrespecting one of my best friends I have ever had, if I tried. His hospital stays, long treatments are nothing that I or most can relate to. However, the pains of watching those you love suffer and struggle is indescribable. By God's grace, Mike is now healthy and so many other memories we shared prevail in my mind, overshadowing those of his sickness. He is a testament to human spirit and his recovery as well as those that he has touched and inspired makes him triumphant. Mike is not perfect and like all falls short, but I know that before his work here on earth is done, he will have touched so many with his story, his integrity, and his silent ways that are a reflection of the most high God.

—James Colman
Michael's best friend in Fredericksburg, Virginia

"Michael has been one of my most inspiring patients. He has suffered some of the most serious complications, but he came through all of them remaining the same sweet, strong young man that he was at the beginning of the journey. It was an honor to take care of such an amazing young man and to work with his family. I think the strong bond between Michael and his mother is one of the main reasons that he was able to withstand all that he did and come through victorious."

—Kimberly P. Dunsmore, M.D.
Hematology/Oncology: Pediatric
University of Virginia Hospital, Charlottesville, VA
Michael's hematology doctor who treated him for leukemia

"Michael Brandon Miller...when I think of that name the thoughts that immediately come to mind are Ramen Noodles in a glass bowl, shy and quiet, will only eat shaved lunch meat, tattoos, humble, Bob Marley, art, must be in excruciating pain before he will bother someone for medicine, Christ loving, Mama's boy (that's a good thing), and peaceful. I could go on and on but the thing that has always struck me about Michael is that no matter what battle he was fighting at the time whether it be cancer, pancreatitis, etc., there was always a peace when I was with him. Instead of me, his nurse, making him feel better, he was always the one making me feel better.

When I first met Michael, he was in the hospital with Leukemia. He was (and still is) shy and quiet, so nice that he would never push the call bell because he "didn't want to bother anyone." Therefore, I always made it a point to check on him a little more often to make sure he was okay. I've never had cancer but one thing I can tell you about it is that IT SUCKS!!! It's not fair to be stuck in the hospital when your friends are out having a good time, it's not fun to be poked and prodded, etc. As a nurse, I have always tried to make the hospital as much fun as possible. If you're going to have to be there then let's make it as much fun as we can. Since Michael was a teenager I wanted to get on his level and find something that he liked. I did try a few things like bringing in my guitar to play for him even though I could only play one cord. However, since I didn't know much about Bob Marley or art, I decided to share with him the one thing that I did know. I knew that as horrible as Leukemia was that God was in control. I shared with him how God knew every hair on his head before he was even born (Mathew 10:30), that He knew Michael would have Leukemia and this was somehow in God's perfect plan. God had already planned and determined the rest of his life and how it would play out. I wanted Michael to know this because I wanted him to quit worrying and just rest in the fact that God was in control. I didn't know how the story would end but I knew that God was holding Michael in the palm of his hands and carrying him through this journey.

Through Michael's illness, there were many times I would leave him not knowing how his story would turn out. We spent several hours in his room over the course of his hospitalizations talking about God and his plan. I couldn't ever promise Michael that he was going to be healed but what I could promise was that either way, he would win in the end. Of course, we didn't want to loose him but I wanted him to also know that Heaven was far beyond his best day here on earth. In Heaven there is no cancer, no pain, no central lines, no sadness- it is perfect, pure, and magical ALL the time! It was important for him to know that because I didn't want him to fear the future no matter how it turned out.

There were a few times after his cord blood transplant that I got a call from Freda telling me to come to Duke to say goodbye. I would cry the entire trip up there and every time he would miraculously bounce back and come out stronger than before. Michael always tries to say that I was the one that lifted him up but in fact, it is just the opposite. Michael is the strongest person I know. Not only did he beat cancer, survive a cord blood transplant and all the complications that go along with it, but he never let any of that change him. He never got mad, tired of fighting, or bitter. He just sat quietly in his room, was polite to everyone that came his way, and held on for the ride. I have learned a lot from Michael and I think I am a better person just from knowing him.

When I think of Michael now, I think of a true angel on earth. He is a miracle to me and he is the perfect example of how God truly is in control. There were so many times the odds were against Michael and yet he not only beat cancer but he has come out stronger than ever. He is such a kind and giving person and I can only hope that someday I can give back to him what he's given to me.

I love you Michael and Freda and I want to thank you for not only allowing me to be your nurse but also a part of your journey!"

—Melissa
Michael's favorite nurse during his hospital stays at UVA and a dear friend

"The things I remember about Michael are when Dr. Dunsmore said there was a young man upstairs that looked like Jesus. The first time he came down to get sedated we were all looking at him and saying to each other, "He does look like Jesus!"

I loved to hear him speak of Bob Marley and show me pictures

of his art. Every time he comes to the hospital, he stops by to see us!
I am so proud of him and that he is doing well."

—Gwendolyn Porterfield,
One of Michael's nurses at the Hematology Clinic

"I remember Michael as an amazingly strong and brave young
man who always helped us to take care of him. He was always willing to push himself as well as accept the things, like the renal failure,
that he could not change. I will always remember him coming to
the clinic in his cowboy hat looking like he didn't have a care in the
world-and yet he was still having to go through dialysis and more
medical care than I would want to go through."

—Paul L. Martin, M.D., Ph.D.
Division Chief, Pediatric Blood and Marrow Transplantation
Duke University Hospital, Durham, N.C.
One of Michael's doctors from his cord blood transplant

Dear Mike,
As I've come to know you, I've been in awe of your inner strength
God has placed in you. Your faith in God and God's plan for your
life has grown with each adversity and trial. Mike, you are the youth
of Isaiah 40:29-31: "He gives power to those who are tired and worn
out; he offers strength to the weak. Even youths will become exhausted, and young men will give up. But those who wait on the
Lord will find new strength. They will fly high on wings like eagles.
They will run and not grow weary. They will walk and not faint."

Mike, God has blessed you for waiting on Him. Enjoy the new
strength, the high flight, the fast run and the brisk walk of life God
has given you.

Love you in Christ,

Bob
—A friend and spiritual mentor who Michael met in Florida

"Michael came to the first class of my Fall Physical Education and sat quietly taking in all the academic speech I have to give at the beginning of every semester. During my first class spiel, I frankly explain to the students that my class is like a military boot camp, we start at the beginning level but I quickly bring up the intensity to an intermittent/advanced fitness level class. Sweating is mandatory and if they are "allergic" to physical exertion of any kind, then they need not waste their time nor mine because this class is not for them. I do ask that they tell me all of their physical limitations, normally, which frankly are things like high blood pressure, diabetes, knee or other joint issues that I can help the student learn to modify around while still being able to take the class.

So at the end of the class, Michael came to me and explained that he had had a pancreas, kidney and bone marrow transplant in the last 10 years and was not sure about being able to take my class. After my initial shock at his revelation, I started to quickly go through my own training knowledge trying to pull out what I knew about working with a person who had had an organ transplant (let alone three), and the effects of anti-rejection drugs and so on. Needless to say, I had nothing...nada...I really had no clue if someone with Michael's medical history should take a class like mine! I was honest about my lack of knowledge but made him a deal to do the research on my end but I asked him to please talk to his doctors, honestly, explain to them about the intensity of my class and ask for their recommendations.

Michael was sick though for the next 3 classes and even though I initially thought that perhaps he decided not to take my class, he called me and told me he was sick with the flu but had definitely decided to take my class. I made several "consulting" phone calls to a couple of my colleagues in the fitness industry as well as researching several websites they recommended. Frankly, neither my colleagues nor the research proved to be very helpful regarding information on exercise and anti-rejection medicines or organ transplants, so I was left with my own experience and common sense. I was very interested to hear what Michael's doctors said but after he talked to them, they basically said he could do what he felt he was physically capable of and the bottom line was that it was up to Michael and me to figure out what he could do!

Honestly, I was very nervous about working with Michael and I am not sure if he sensed that or not but his demeanor is so calming that I took my cues from him! I teased him that I had visions of his kidney or pancreas exploding out of his body after I had him do some particular exercise! He just chuckled and said "Well, you never know!"

So we decided he would pace himself during class, push his body as much as he could and back off as it was necessary and if there was a particular exercise we were doing that I felt was contraindicated to his body, he could modify himself. What was impressive to me was how subtly he would conduct his modifications so that no one around him really paid any attention and therefore he never called attention to himself. In this manner, he really became my hero because while some of my other very healthy students were whining and complaining about how much they "hated" whatever exercise we were doing at the time, here is Michael in class pushing his body to do things I knew were a struggle for him but yet he persevered! I wanted to yell at these crybabies – "Look at Michael! If he can do this, why can't you!?" I did not do this in this class because I wanted to respect his unspoken desire to just be one of the "regular" students. I did, however, use Michael's story to inspire my other PE class and my personal training clients!

In my future classes as well as my own personal life, I will use Michael's story of persevering through some of the most difficult medical struggles I have ever heard about and then to be able to push his body to not only get through such an intense physical fitness class but to do so in such an outstanding manner. In my mind it is a true testimony to the strength of his will and character! I hope to stay in touch with Michael and monitor his success in life because I have no doubt that he WILL succeed in any way he wants!"

—Patrice S. DeBord, Adjunct Professor
Physical Education Department
Germanna Community College

"Seems like a lifetime already since Michael was going through his cancer and treatments. But I am still always amazed how Michael carried himself through those dark days. I will never forget receiving the phone call that Michael had cancer. That same day I received the news that my mother-in-law had passed away. It was a very sad day for our family.

Over the next years I would eagerly wait for updates about Michael's condition. It seemed like he was on a roller coaster ride with his disease. Initially, I was very scared for him because it was so serious. I remember being told about some intense treatments he had to have. Eventually he was doing better and I would marvel at the stories coming from Freda and Randy. He had to stay home from school and be tutored, but his classmates showed how much they cared and did fundraisers for him. These stories touched my spirit and I was glad he was so loved by his friends. Then there was news the cancer came back. I can't imagine how Michael felt, but I know it made me sick to think he would have to go through treatments again. I wasn't around Michael very much because I live in Georgia, so I didn't see the struggles he had to face. I would call to check on him and through the phone calls I would hear about Michael trying to stay positive and this would keep me encouraged. Freda was a rock for Michael, she was there with him every step of the way. Freda and Michael made many trips to UVA hospital and had long stays. Randy would make some trips also, but he was working and watching young Randy at home. My parents were a constant support through all of this. Being long distance, this was a comfort knowing they were all helping the best they could.

The time came for Michael needed to have a cord blood transplant at Duke Hospital. I was hopeful for this procedure and prayed this would give him some normalcy in his life. I was fortunate to visit Michael while he was at Duke. It was a very long stay for him. One day I got a phone call that it didn't look like Michael would make it. I was at church and just started crying. I told all my church friends and they prayed for him. My church family has been praying for Michael for several years, as I know many people were. I believe in the power of prayer and I do think all of the prayers helped Michael through this very difficult trial in his life. Through the miracle of God and the support of the doctors, Michael pulled through.

After years of treatment, which ravaged his organs, Michael, needed a kidney/pancreas transplant. I prayed something would happen quickly. I prayed the cancer would not come back and I prayed that the organs would not cause his demise. Finally, the good news came that he was going to get his transplant. I was so excited and grateful I told everyone that had been praying for Michael. I was nervous that his body would not accept the organs. However, it did and he is alive today and finally attending college, which makes me so happy for him.

Michael went through many changes through this difficult journey. At one point, his hair and face changed quite a bit from the treatment that if I would have seen him on the street somewhere I might not have recognized him. He now looks like a healthy, young adult. But one thing that remained the same is his sweet spirit. He has a gentle, kind way about him. He trusts in God and I believe God has used Michael through this disease to touch so many lives with his kind spirit and encouragement. To hear now that he is doing so well in college and life gives joy to my spirit.

Michael, thanks for your inspiration through the years and I love you."

—Aunt Yvonne

"I will never forget the call I received from my mother. Her words came out so muffled and so disturbing. Michael has leukemia, she said. It is the word you don't ever want to hear within a family. I felt so sick, so helpless, so thoughtless and angry. I wanted questions answered now! Why God, why this sweet, gentle, loving and respectful young man, why? I wanted to take his sickness away at that moment. I assured myself this is not fair, something went wrong, the test must be incorrect this isn't real, I'm dreaming. Then that sick feeling came over me. You know, that one that comes when tragedy hits home. All I could think of is this poor young man and the road ahead. The sick feeling was getting worse. My thoughts for his mom went through me like a tornado, Oh no, Freda! How in the world will this wonderful mom/person be able to cope with this? I couldn't even imagine what Michael and Freda must have felt like inside. I knew these two had such a close bond. Then there is Big Randy and little Randy, how are they going to cope? What is this family to do God?

All I played over and over in my mind is Michael. He is the best teenager I have ever met! Well, the whole family was devastated, lost for words, then came the long, long journey. Michael had to face many hurdles that many people could never overcome. I could not believe the extent of this young mans courage, faith and will to fight for life. He is truly amazing!

I could never imagine everything this family has been through and their will to stay strong.

Many years later and millions of prayers go by and the fight for Michael's life continued. I have seen the struggles and felt the pain for the family. This whole disease took it's toll on everyone who cared about Michael. Our hopes would rise and then fall. Everyone came together for fundraisers. This was the time I wished I could have pulled a miracle from my pocket.

I can't imagine what went on day to day in Michael's life or how his family coped with the stress from it all. I can say the family pulled together and a miracle truly happened, God gave Michael back to us and to see him smile is a true blessing."

—Aunt Melissa

To my son, My miracle.

I love you,

—Mom

Michael Miller in a 2012 photo.

Freda Higgins is an artisan and author currently residing in Reedville, Virginia. Freda and her husband, Randy, have been married for twenty five years and are blessed with two wonderful sons, Michael and Randy Mathew.

CPSIA information can be obtained at www.ICGtesting.com
Printed in the USA
LVOW11s1926240716

497565LV00002B/2/P